Hearts Coloring Book For Adults

Stress Relieving Relaxation Coloring Book
With 40 Heart Inspired Patterns

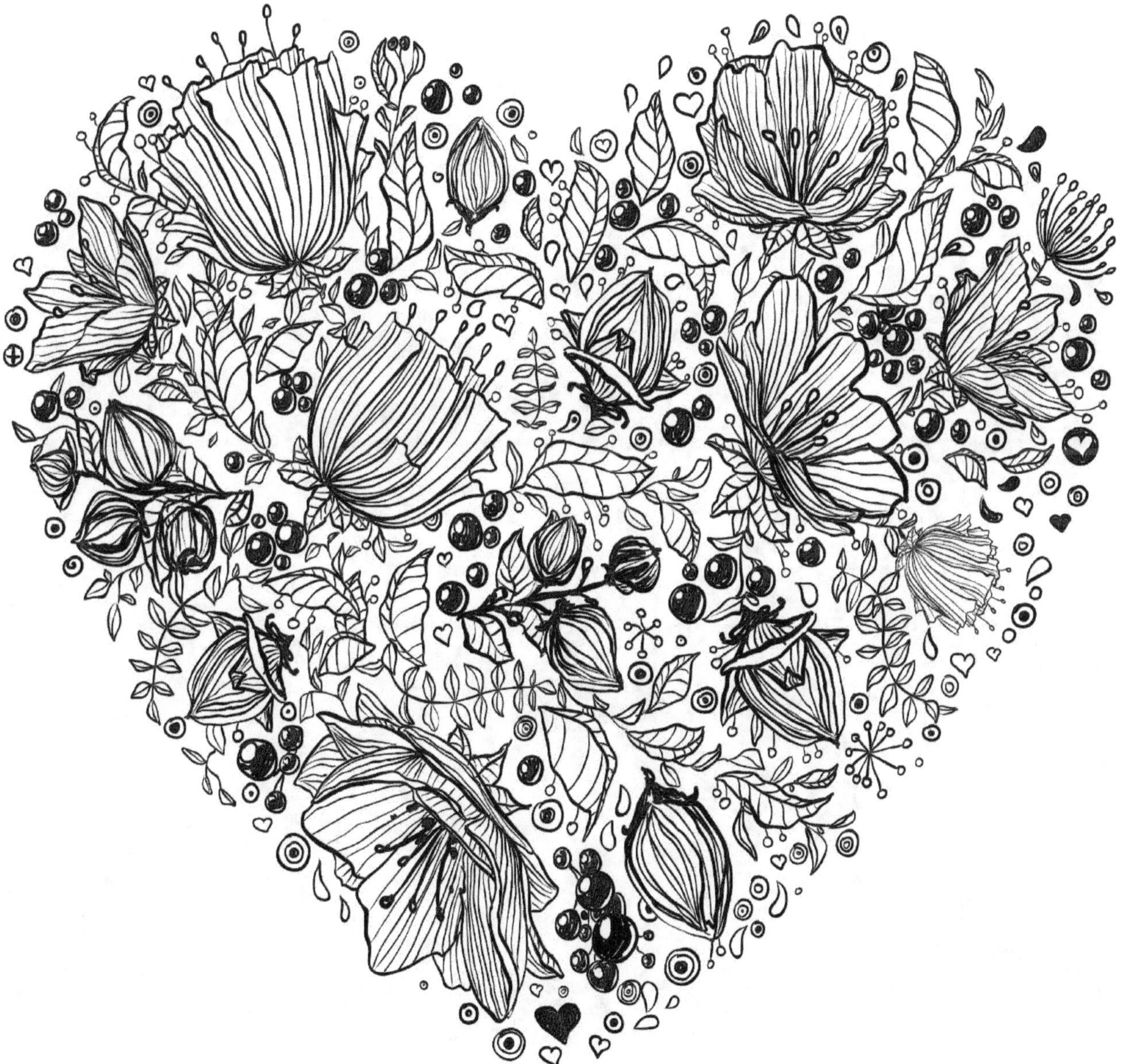

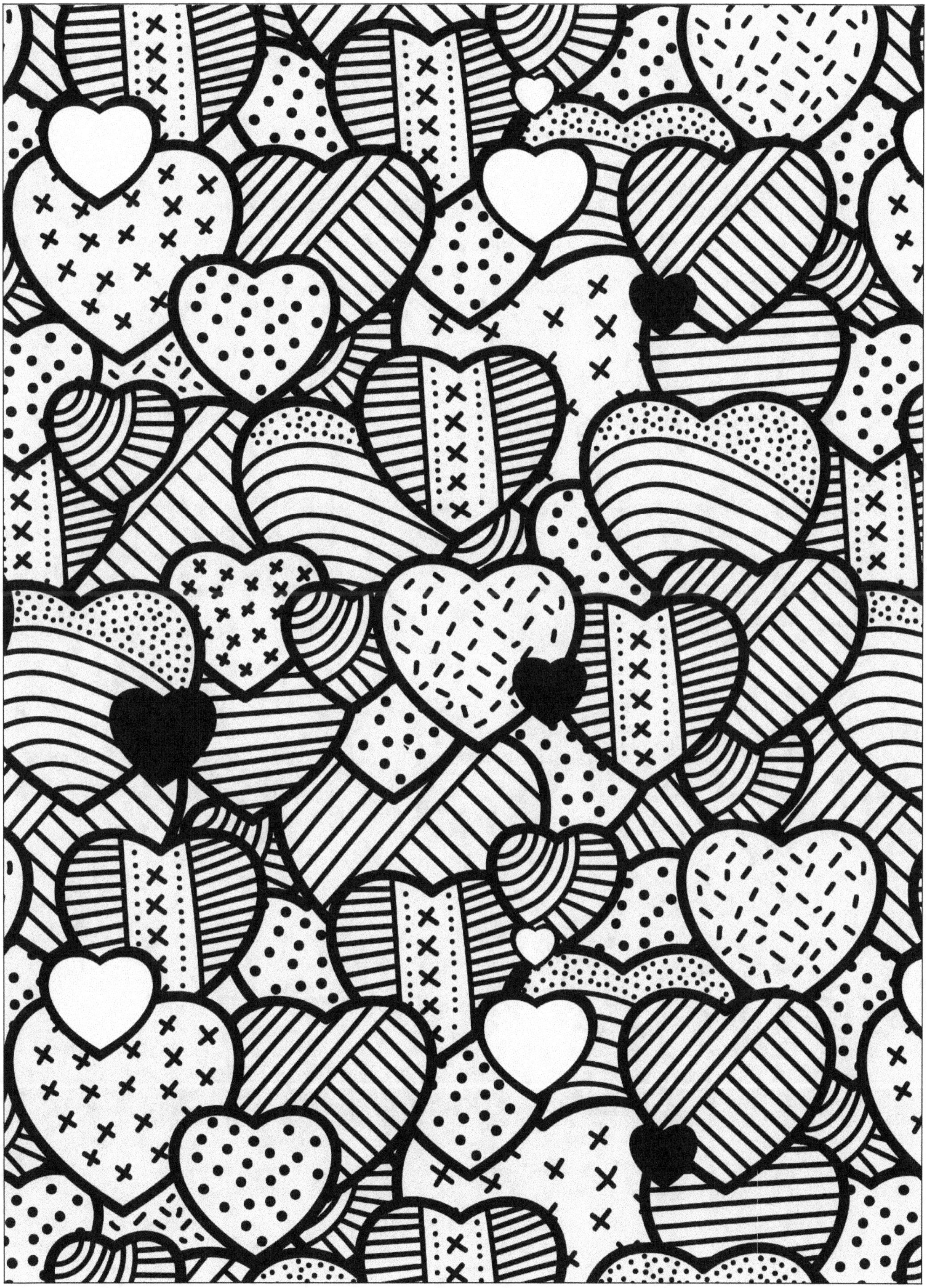

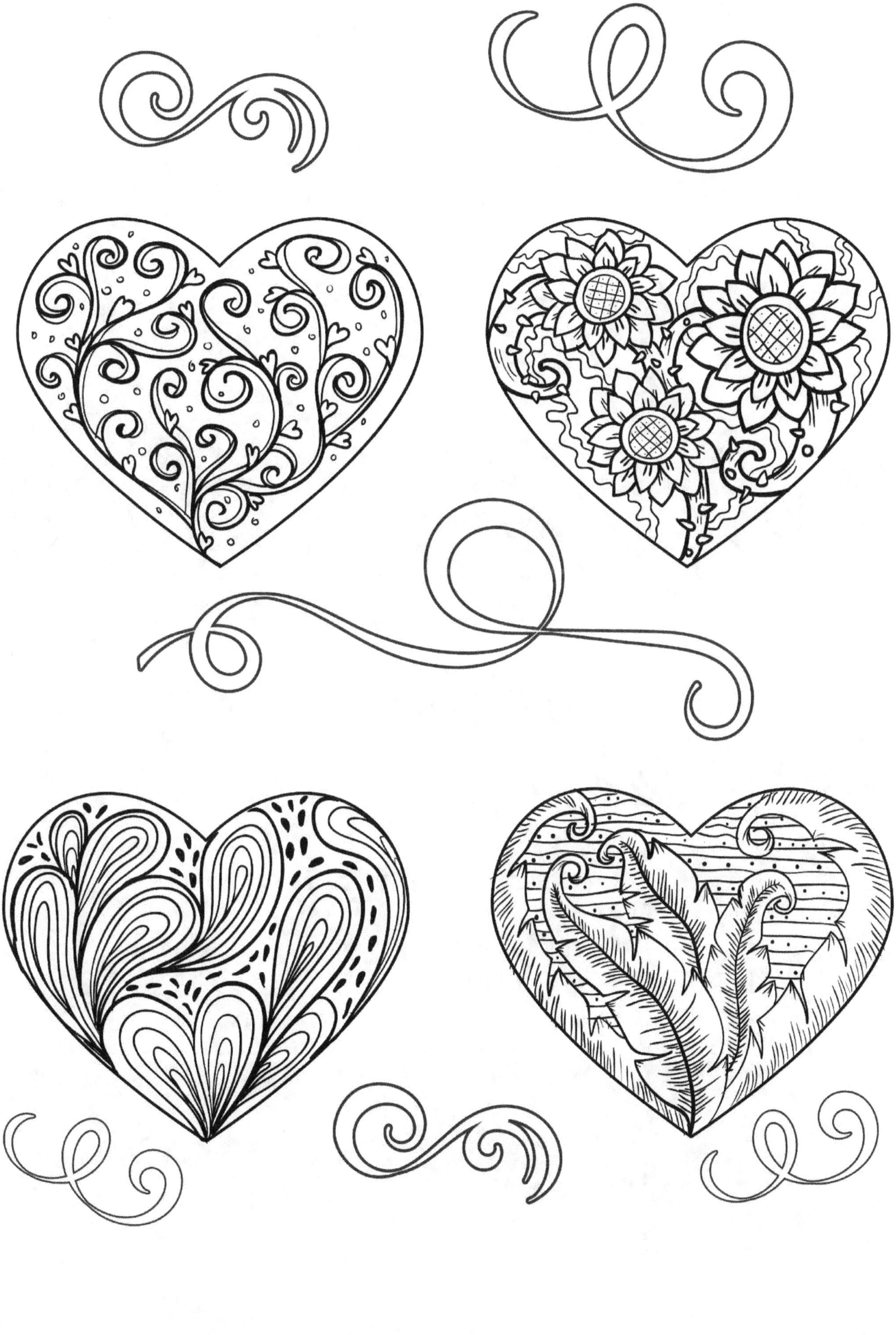

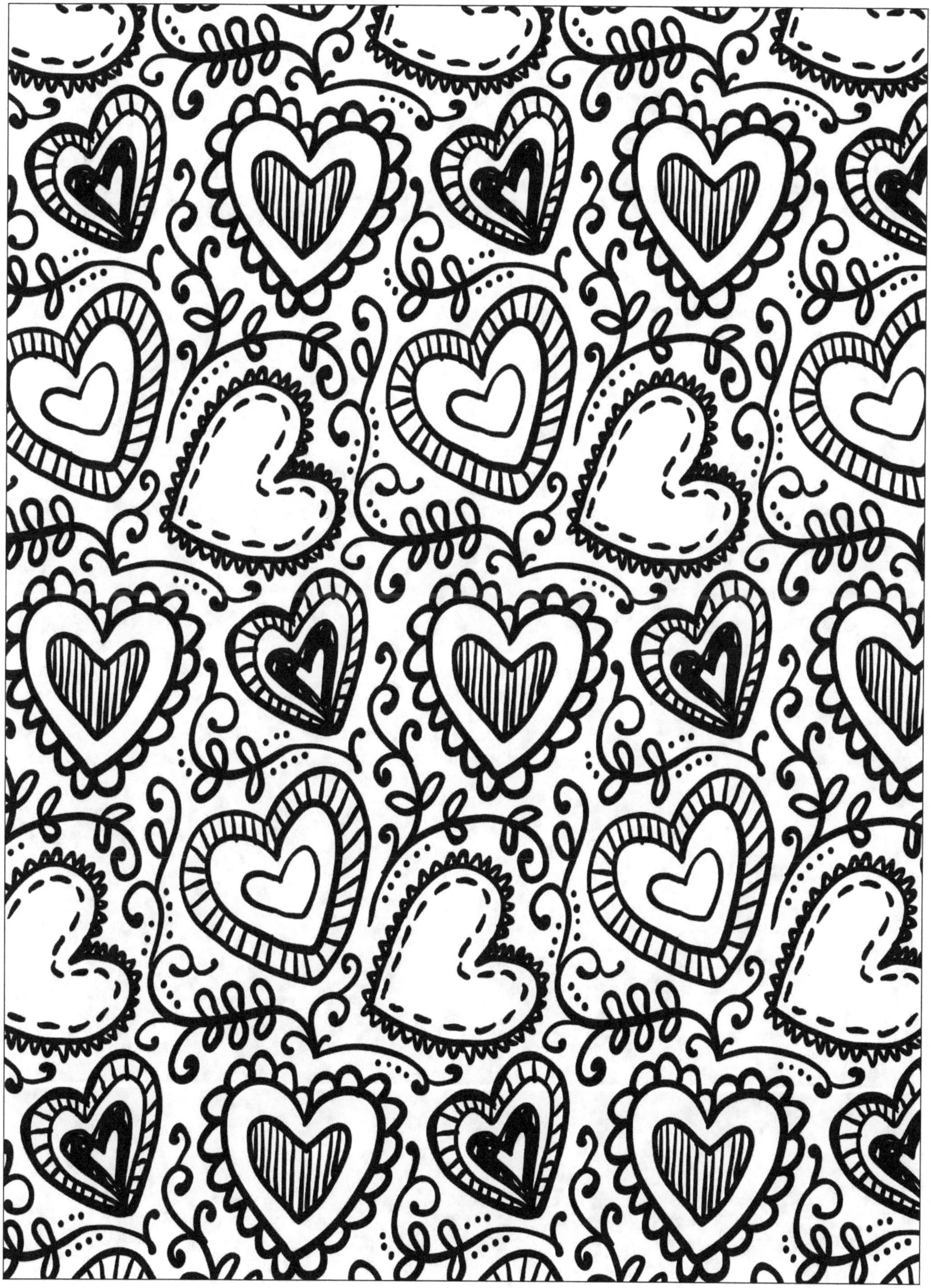

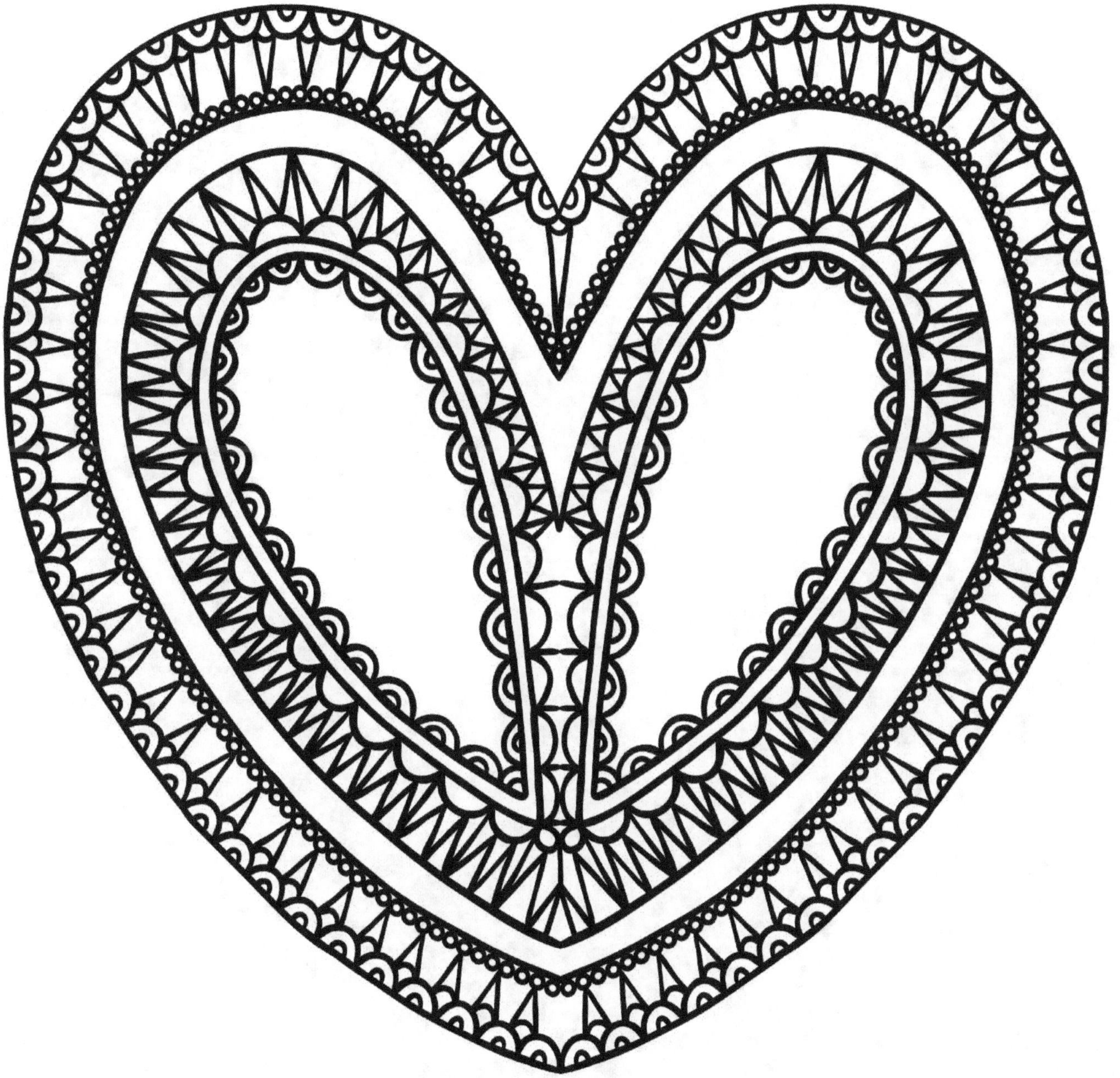

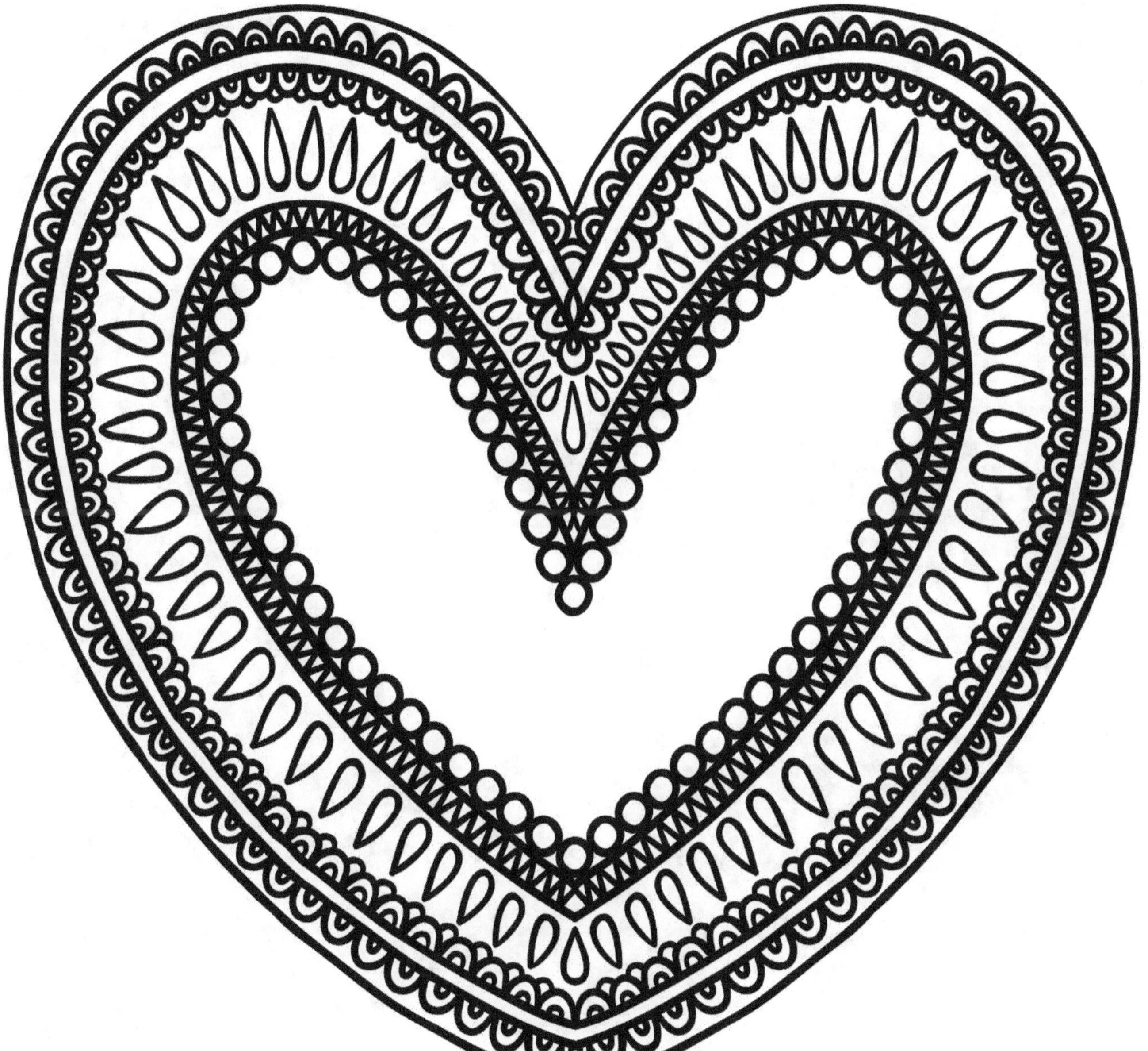

HEARTS
I ♥ U

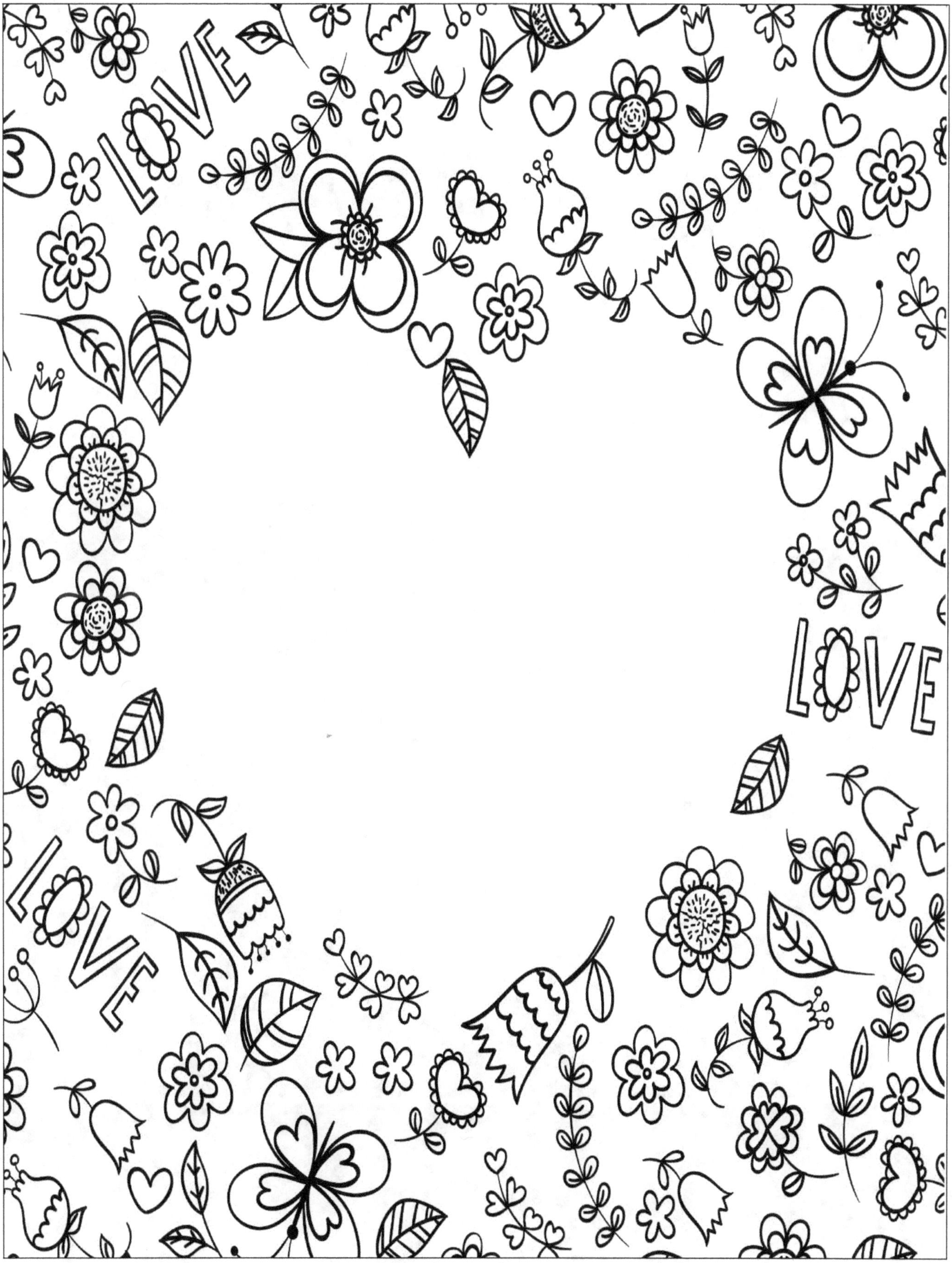
LOVE
LOVE
LOVE

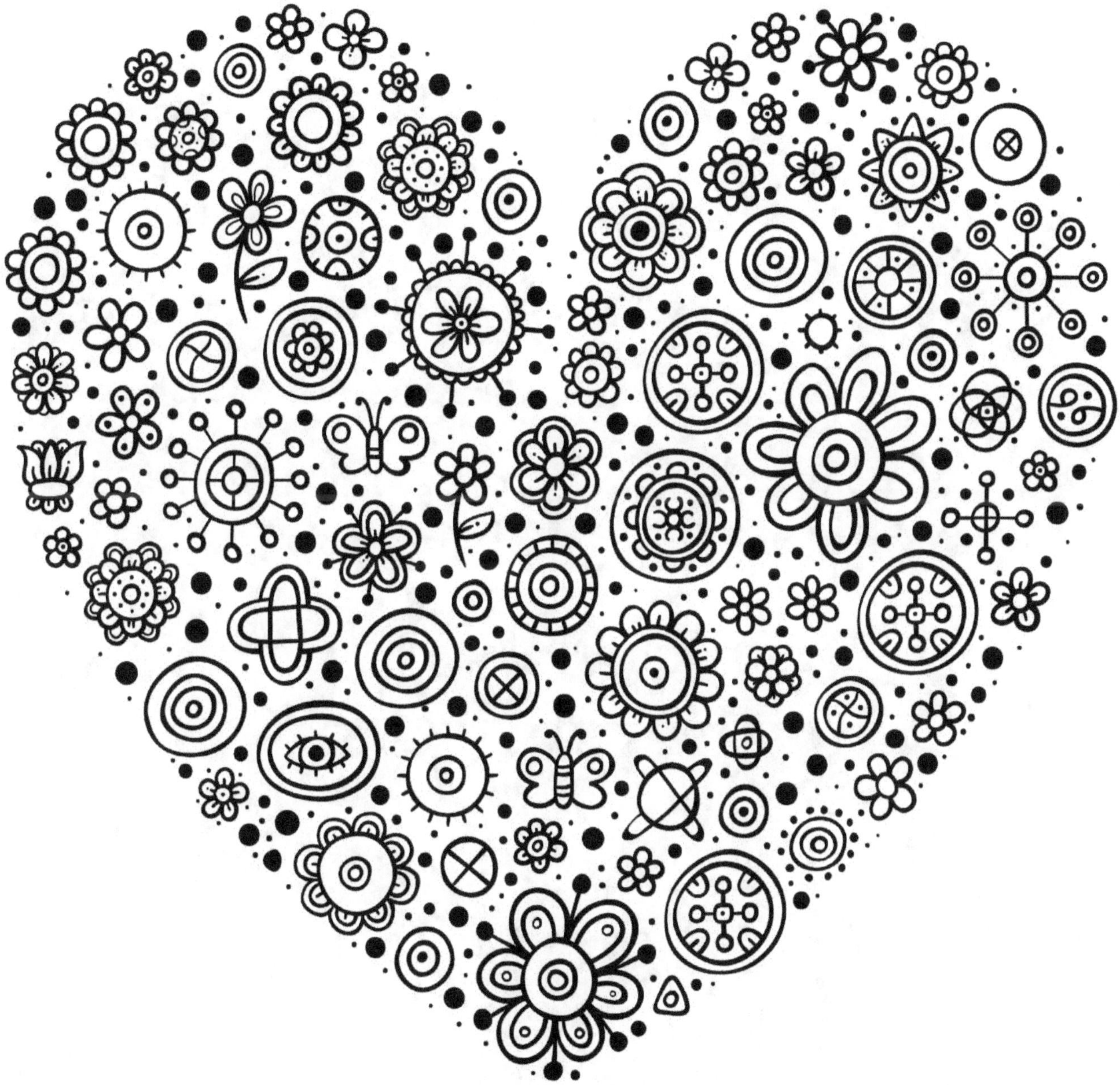

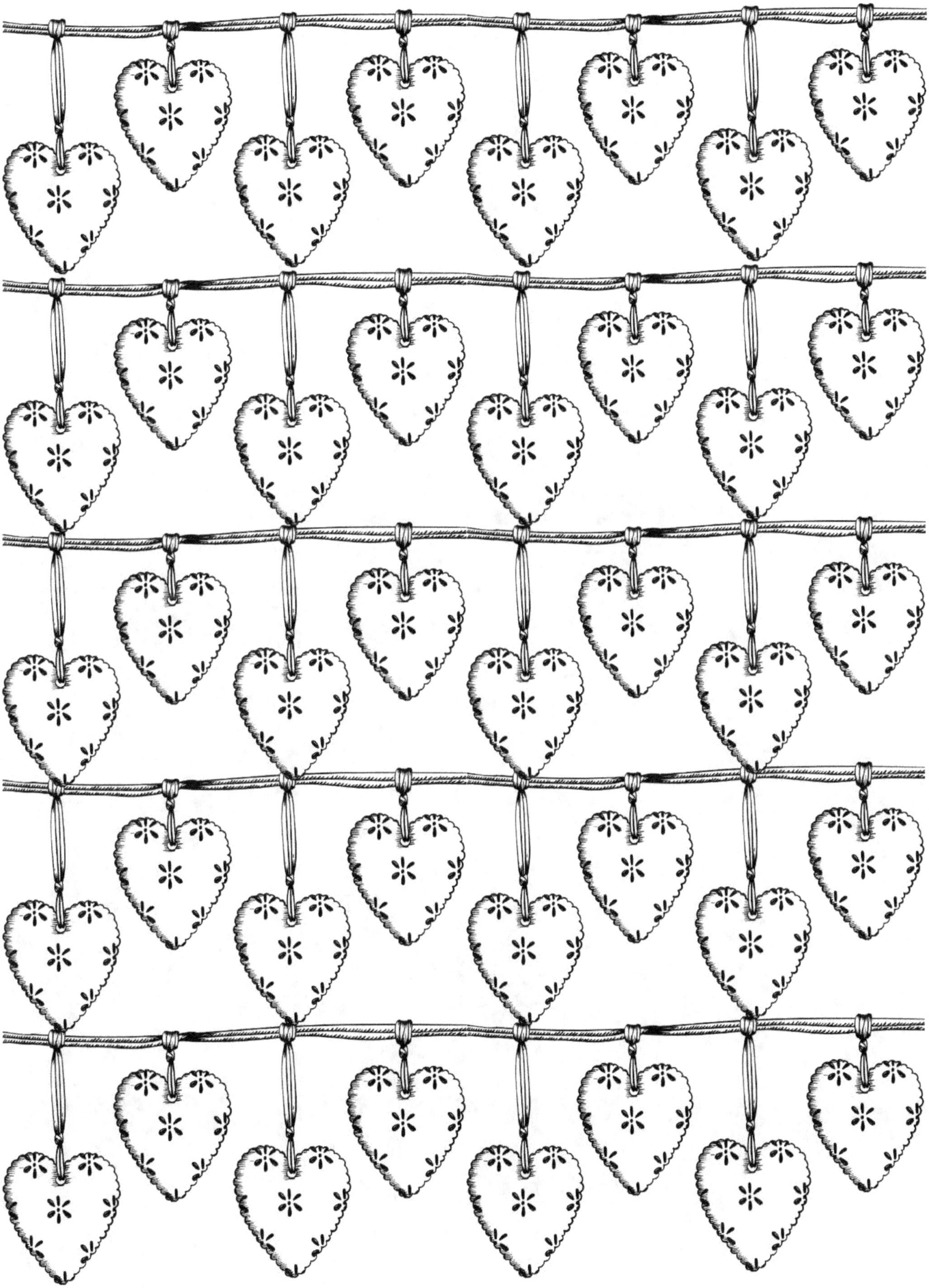

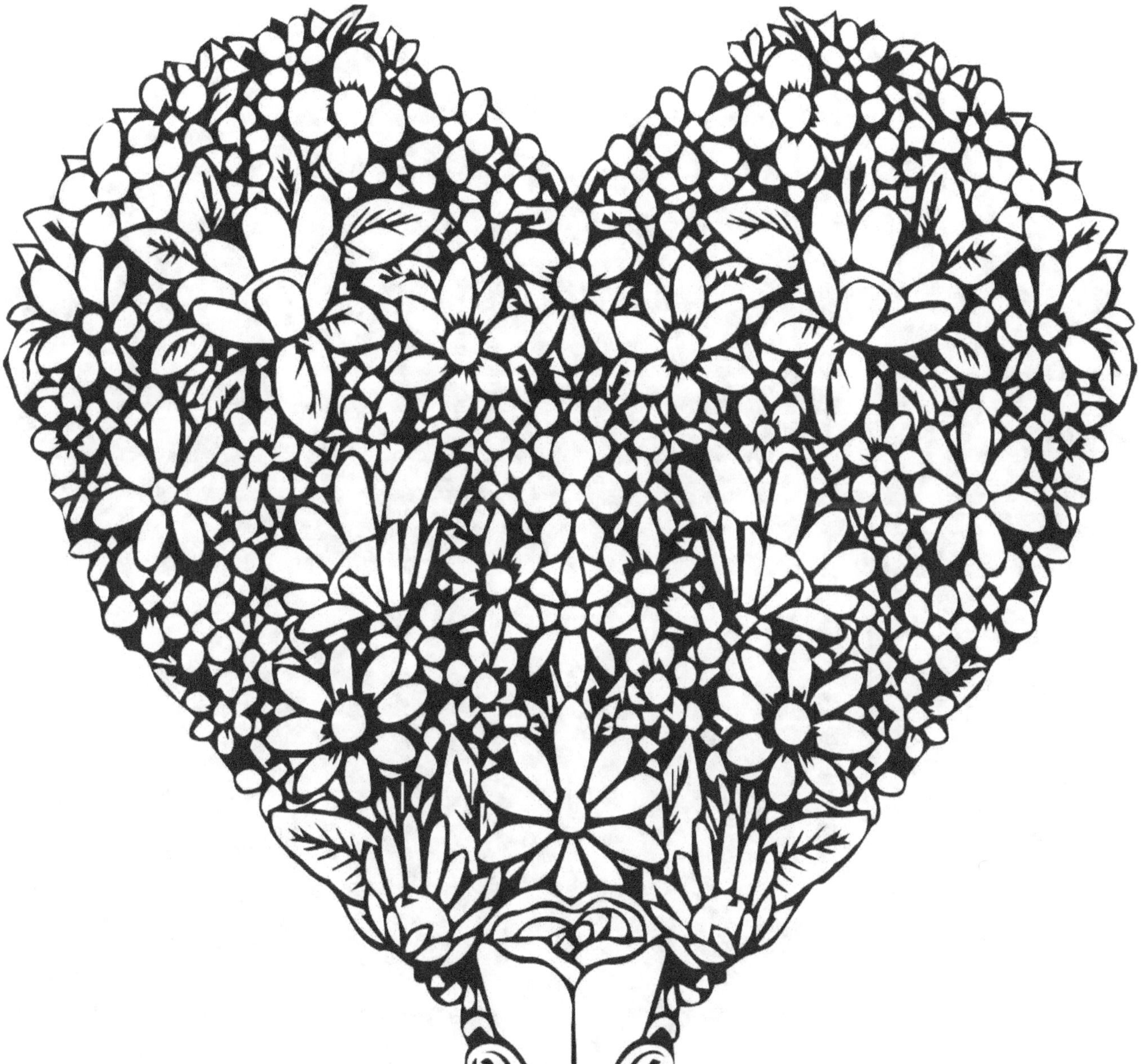

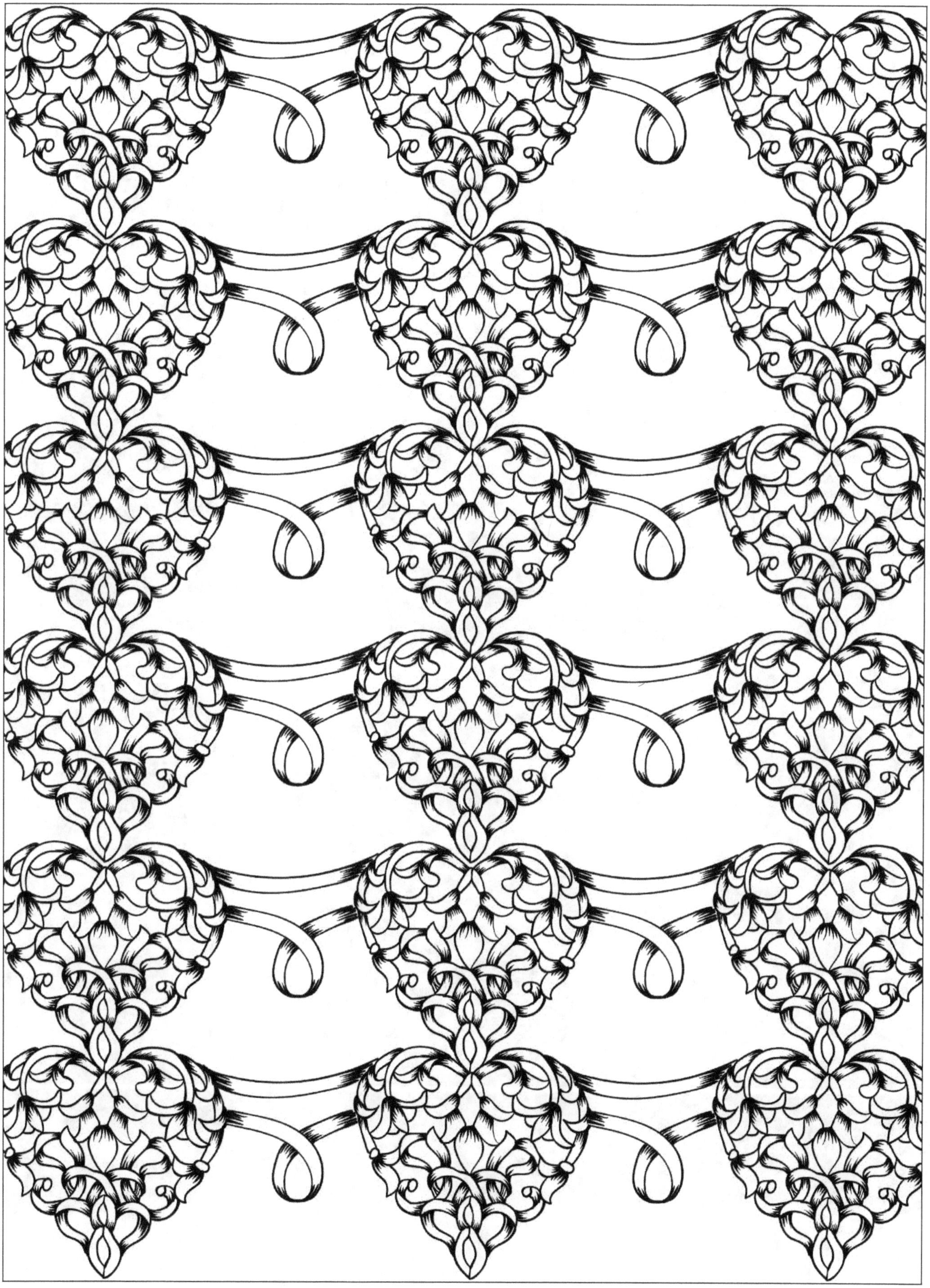

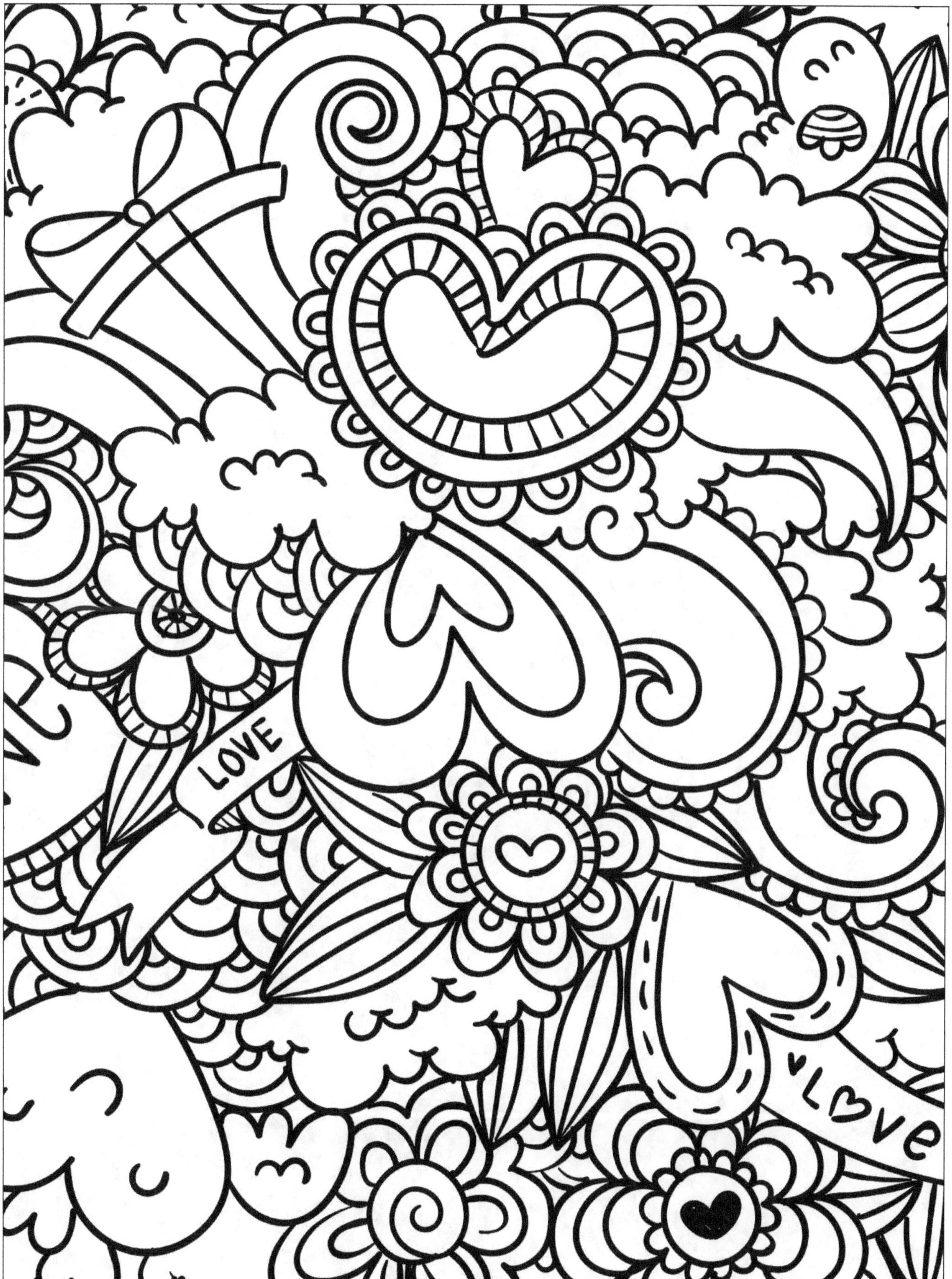
LOVE
Love

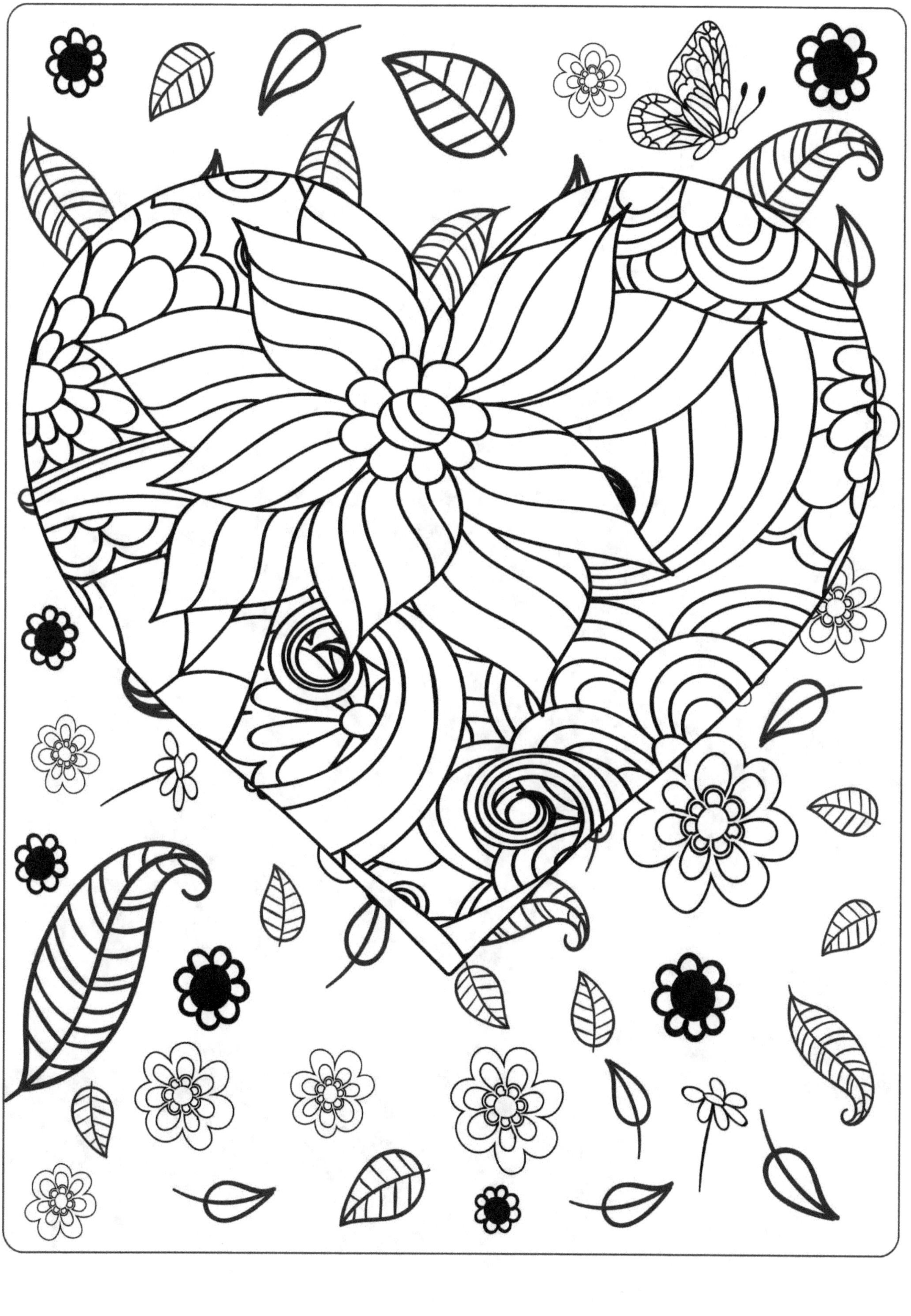

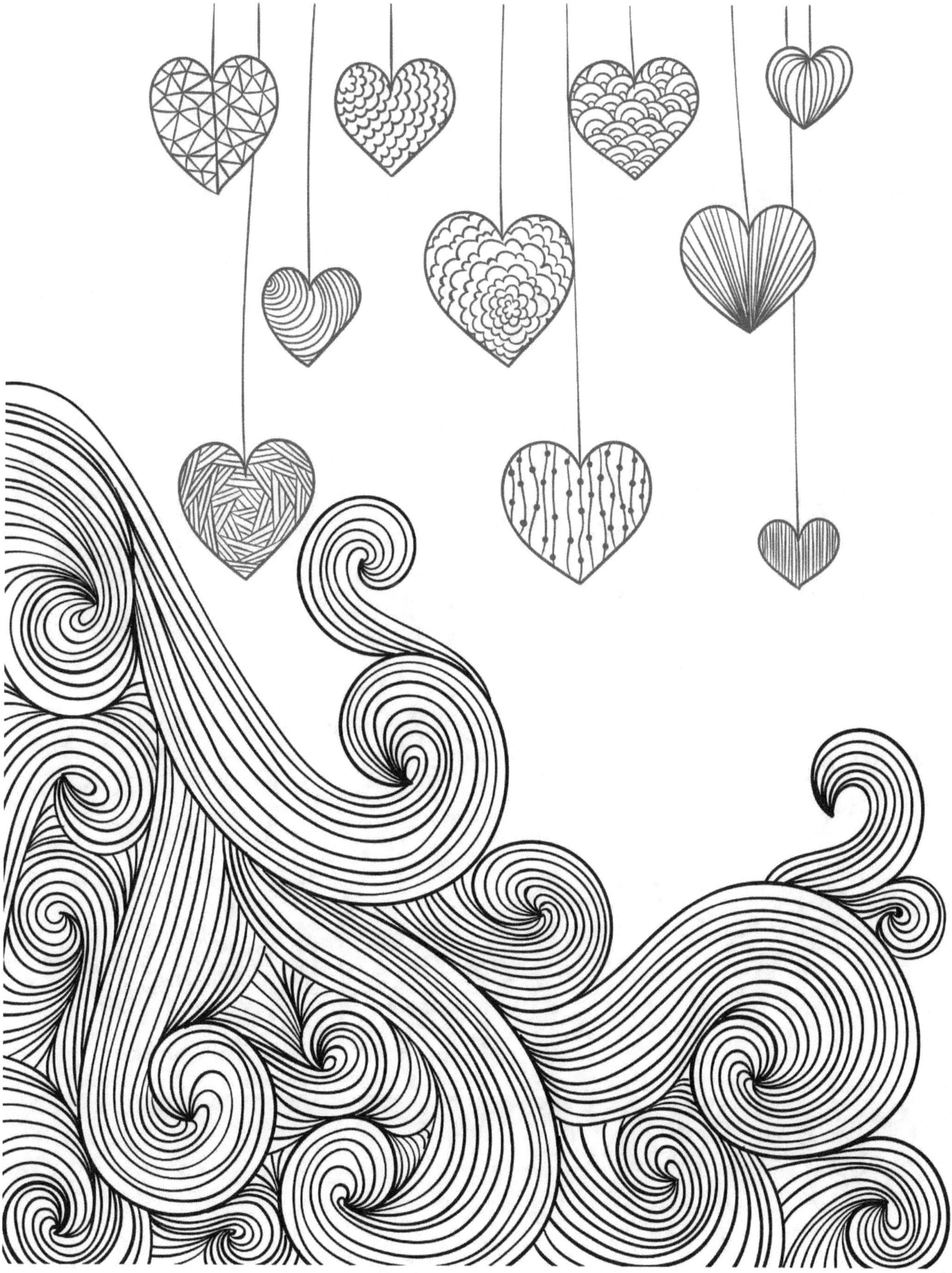

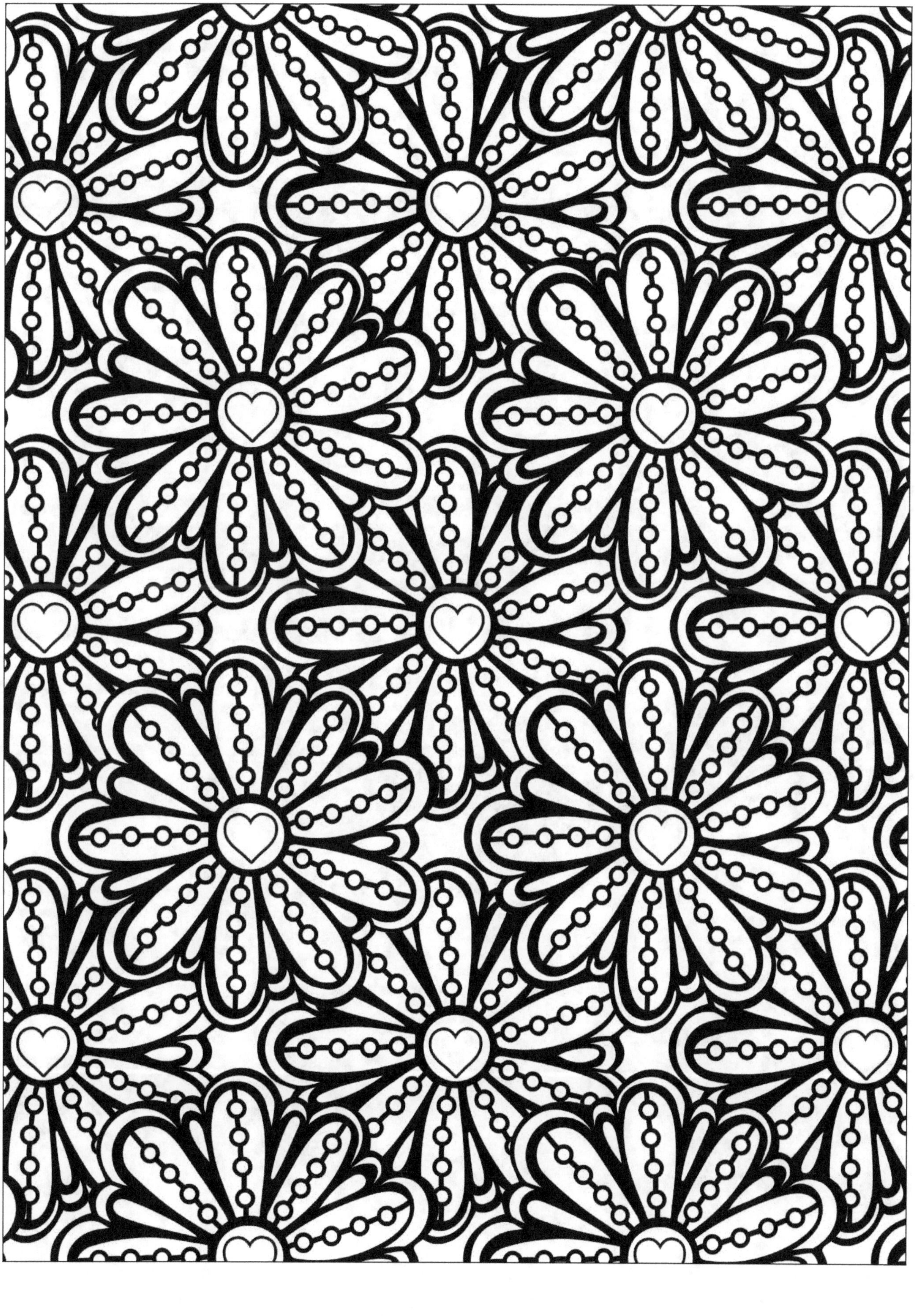

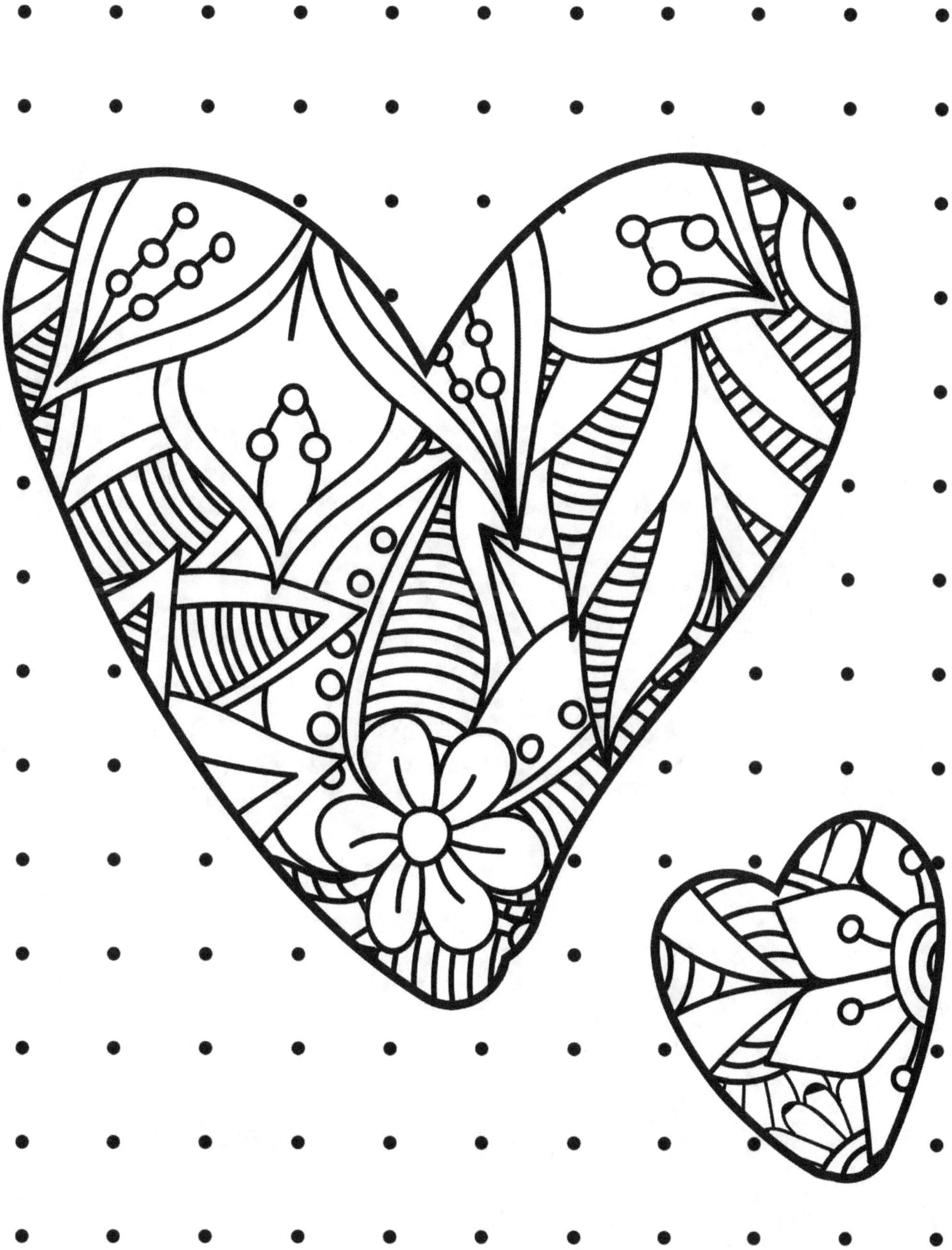

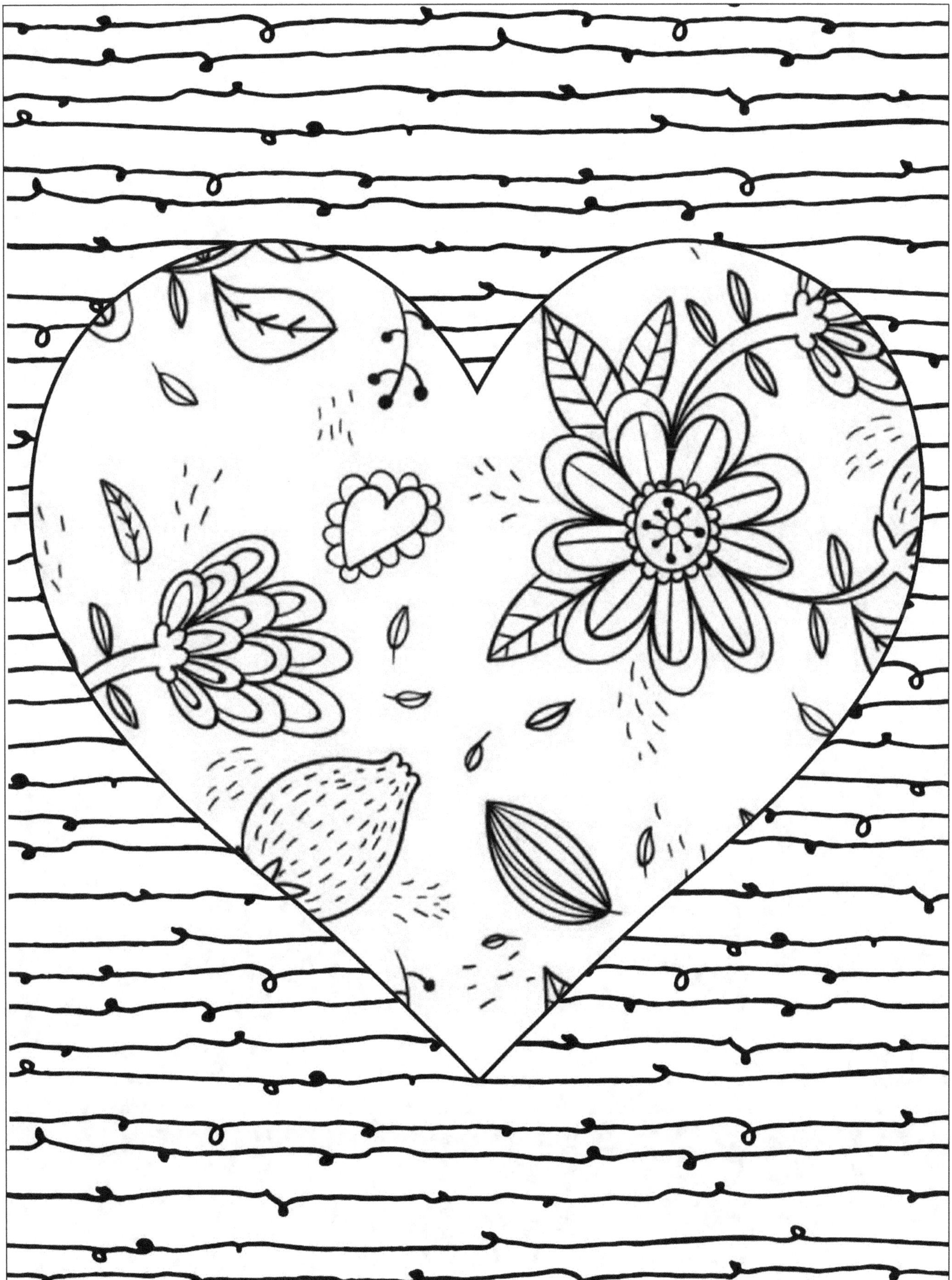

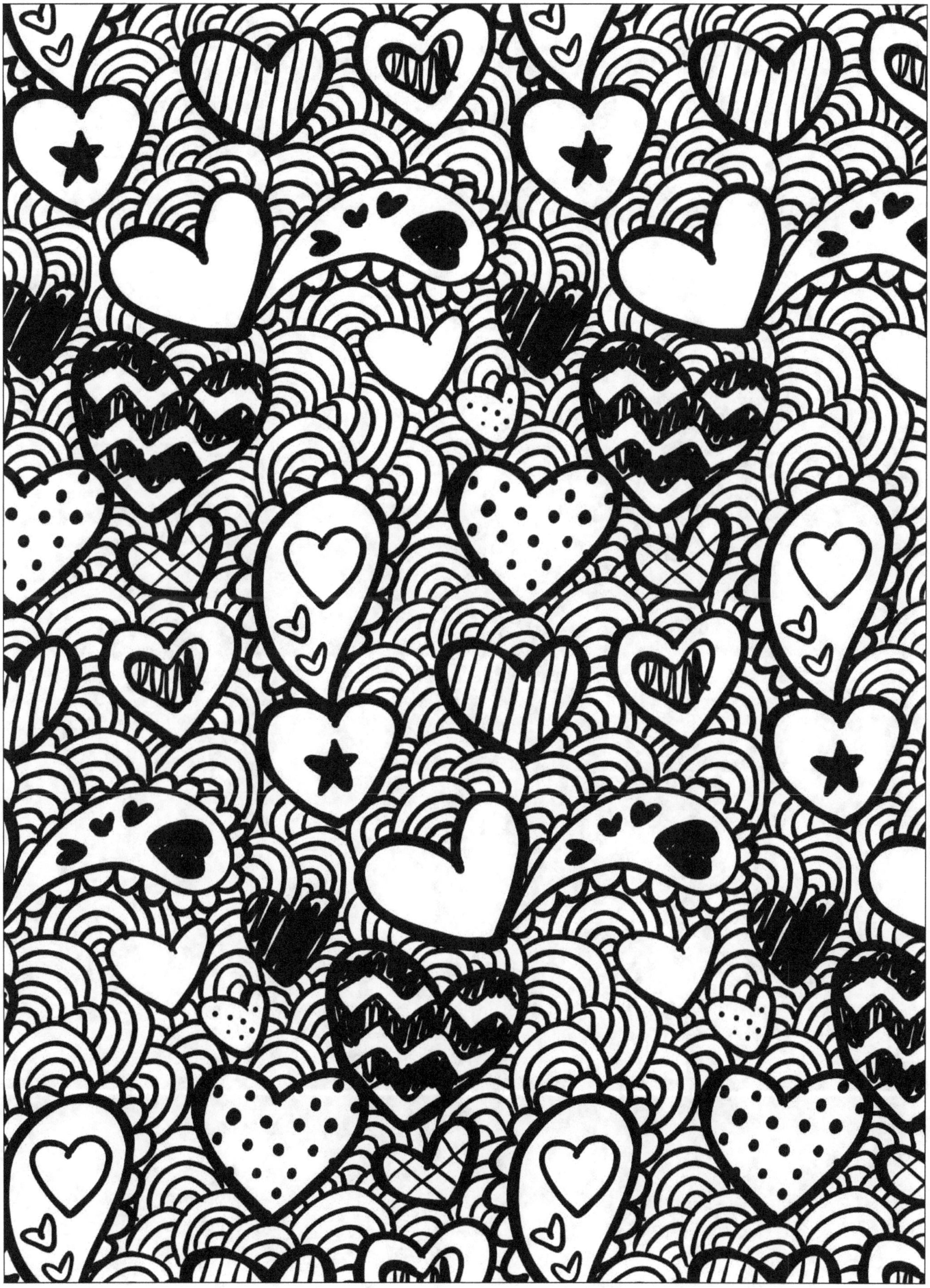

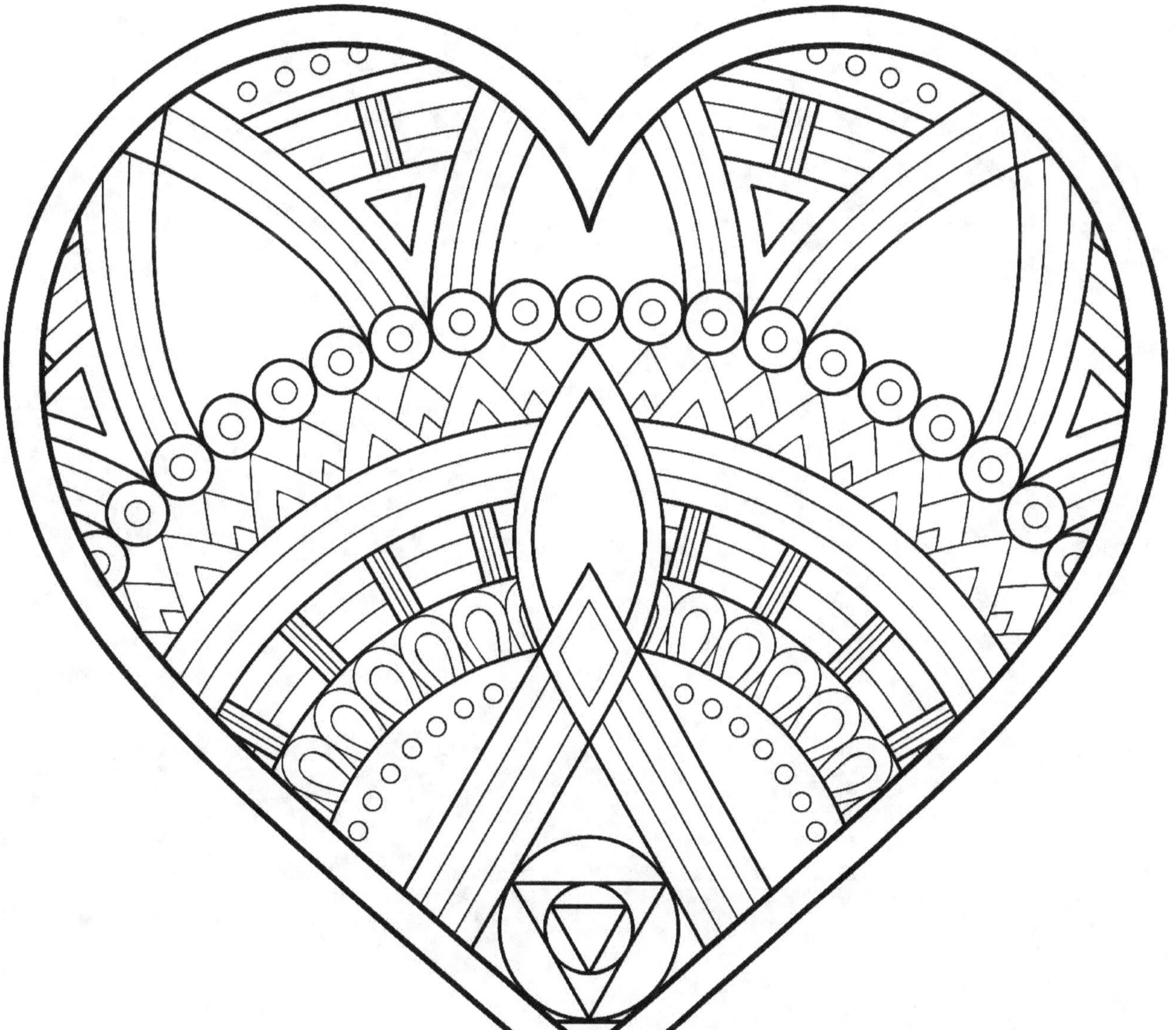

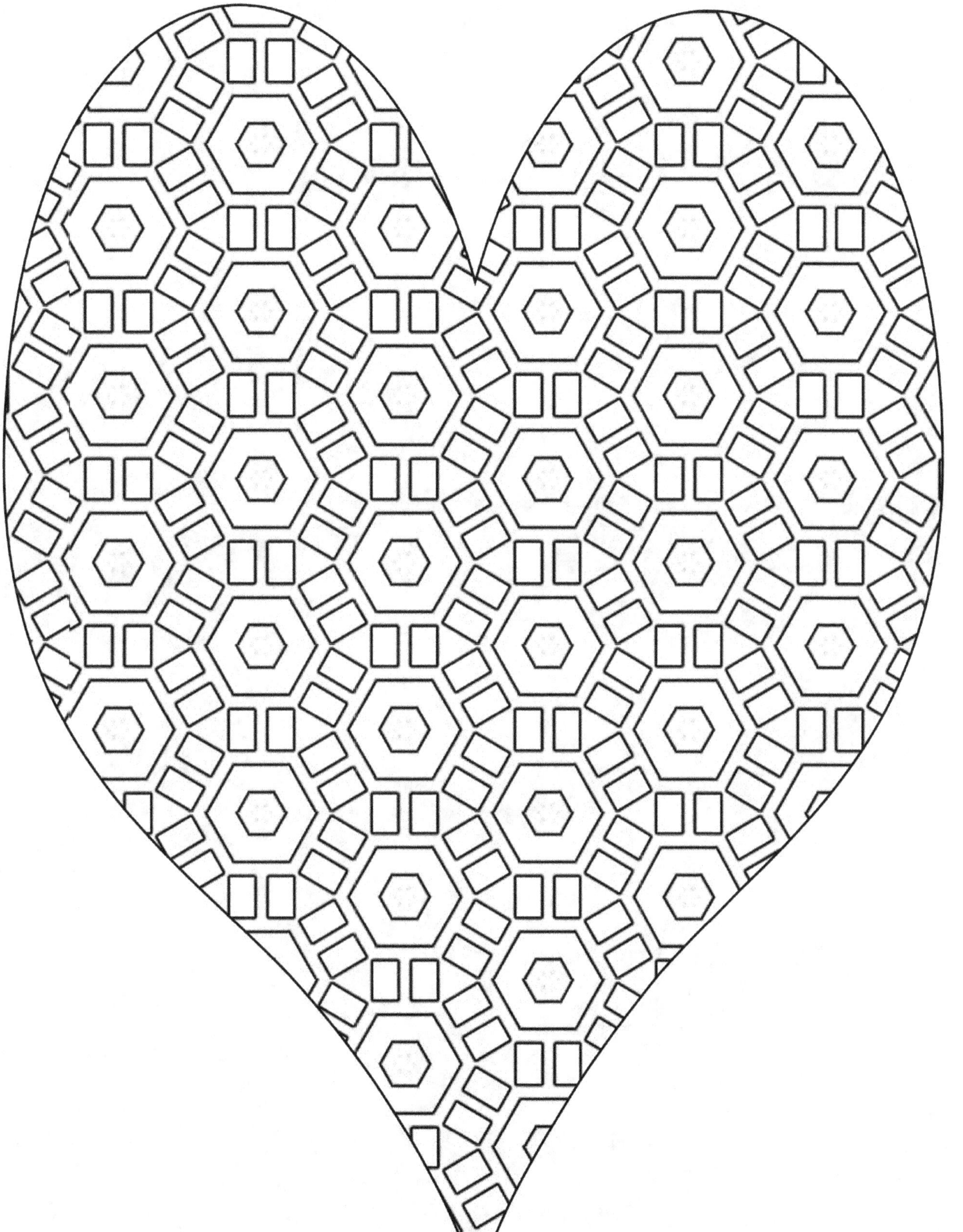

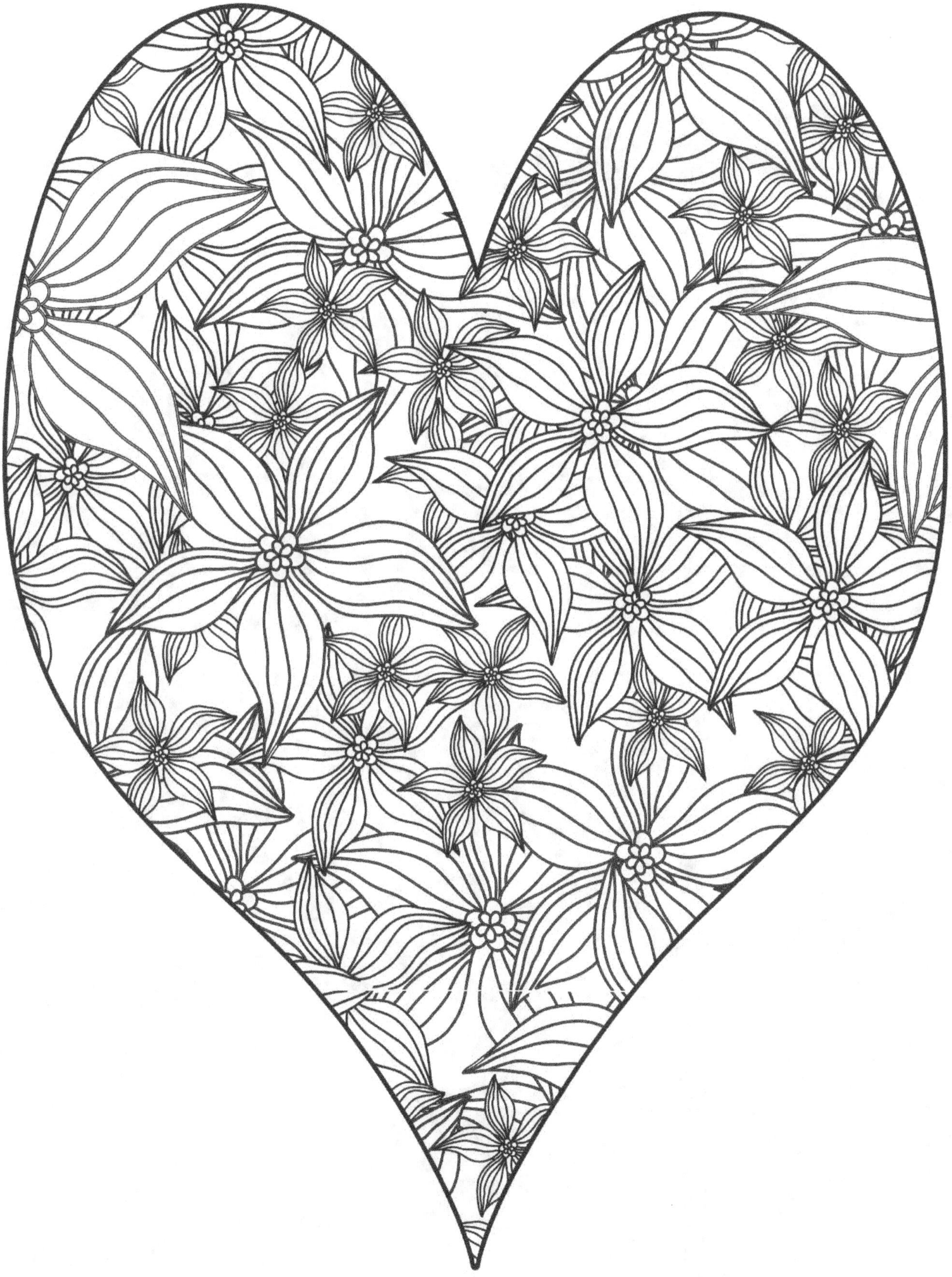

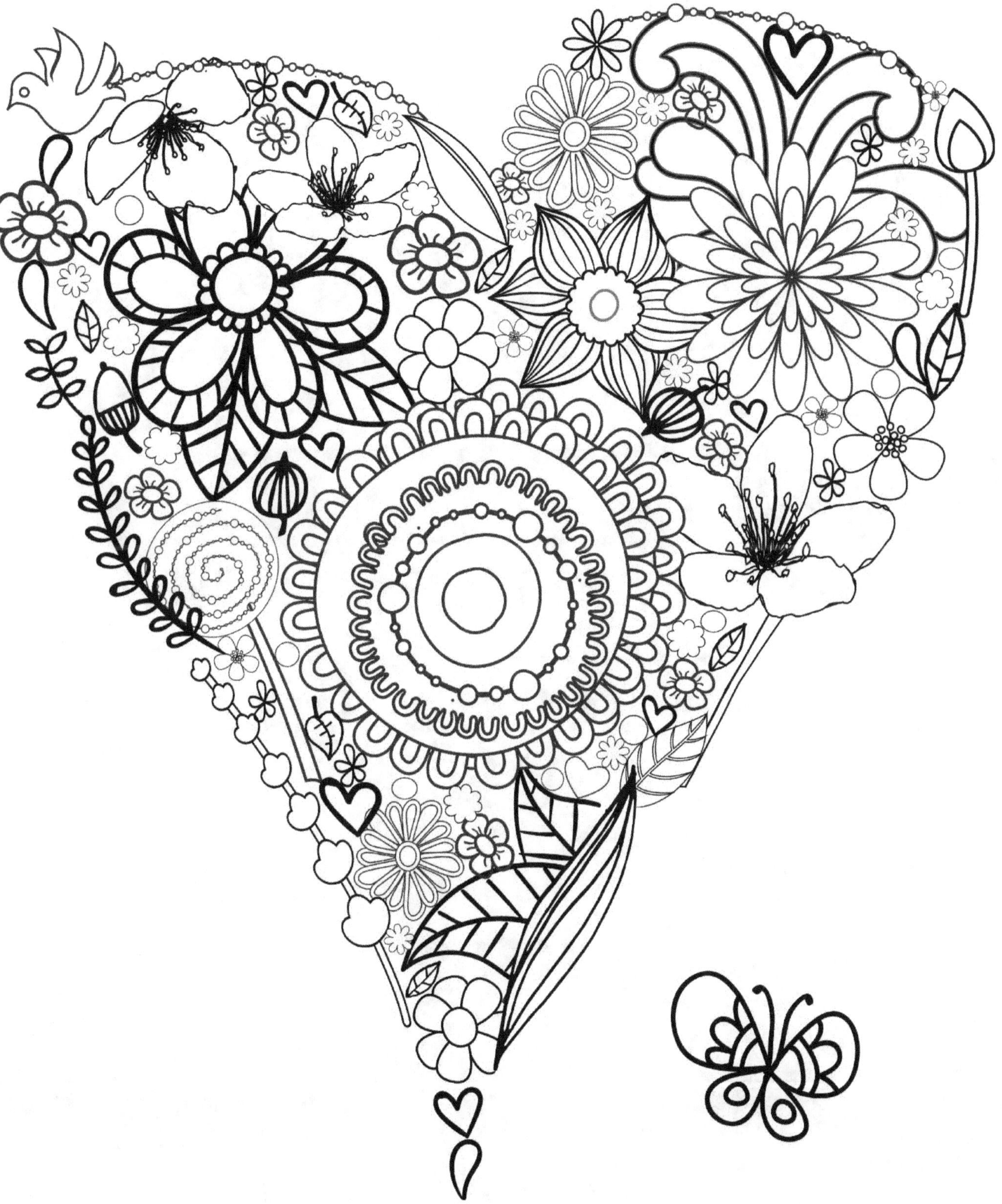

www.ingramcontent.com/pod-product-compliance
Lightning Source LLC
Chambersburg PA
CBHW081842170526
45167CB00007B/2878
* 9 7 8 1 5 4 4 2 3 1 6 5 5 *